THE BALLAD OF YELLOW WEDNESDAY

Emma Must's poems have been published widely in magazines, journals and anthologies in the UK and Ireland. Her debut poetry pamphlet, *Notes on the Use of the Austrian Scythe* (2015), won the Templar Portfolio Award. In 2016, she was named as one of the 'Rising Generation' of poets by *Poetry Ireland Review*, and in 2018 she received an Arts Council of Northern Ireland ACES Award. Her poem 'Toll' won the Environmental Defenders Prize in the 2019 Ginkgo Prize for Ecopoetry. In 2021, she completed a PhD in English at Queen's University Belfast, focusing on ecopoetry and ecocriticism. Formerly a full-time campaigner on environment and development issues, she co-founded the protest group Road Alert! in the early 1990s, then worked for a decade with organisations including ALARM UK, Transport 2000 (now the Campaign for Better Transport) and the World Development Movement. In 1995, she received the Goldman Environmental Prize for Europe. She lives in Belfast.

The Ballad of
Yellow Wednesday

E M M A   M U S T

Valley Press

First published in 2022 by Valley Press
Woodend, The Crescent, Scarborough, YO11 2PW
www.valleypressuk.com

ISBN 978-1-915606-04-4
Cat. no. VP0210

Cover and text design by Peter Barnfather.
Edited by Kate Simpson.

Printed and bound in Great Britain
by TJ Books Limited.

for everybody who tried to save Twyford Down
and in memory of David Croker, Stephen Ward and Alan Weeks

Contents

Here is your road, tying

you to its meanings: gorge, boulder, precipice.

— MURIEL RUKEYSER

For poetry makes nothing happen: it survives
In the valley of its making where executives
Would never want to tamper, flows on south
From ranches of isolation and the busy griefs,
Raw towns that we believe and die in; it survives,
A way of happening, a mouth.

— W. H. AUDEN

Preface

Twyford Down, near Winchester in southern England, was a mile-long hill of chalk in an Area of Outstanding Natural Beauty: the landscape which inspired Keats to write 'To Autumn'. With its Bronze and Iron Age Scheduled Ancient Monuments and two Sites of Special Scientific Interest, this place was, theoretically, protected. But it stood in the way of the 'missing link' of the M3 motorway, designed to shave seven minutes off the journey between Southampton and London.

On Wednesday 9 December 1992 – after years of public inquiries, legal action and campaigning – dozens of security guards wearing fluorescent yellow jackets moved onto the Down, followed by bulldozers, to enable the Department of Transport to begin the main phase of construction work. They were met with resistance by the Dongas Tribe, a small group of young people camped on the hill, who took their name from the ancient trackways on which they lived.

Yellow Wednesday spawned direct action and mass protests against the construction of the road over the next six months, changing the nature of environmental campaigning in Britain.

The protests invigorated a national grassroots movement. This ultimately resulted in the cancellation, by 1998, of all but 37 of the 600-plus road schemes originally proposed by Margaret Thatcher in 1989, described at the time as 'the biggest road-building programme since the Romans'.

I grew up a few miles from Twyford Down, and, in 1992, was working in Winchester Library. I became heavily involved in the protests to stop the road, which included a period of detention in Holloway Prison as one of the 'Twyford Seven'.

This book of poems reflects on that time.

– Emma Must

Chalk, with Flints

Somewhere in the unconscious, the echoed consonants
— Don Paterson

Chock-full of coccoliths under the microscope:
a basket of cartwheels, corpuscles, Coke-bottle caps;
a shingle of cameos. Think of phytoplankton
discarding their skeletons in a warm shelf sea,
quietly as snow, how carbon dioxide spikes
at an absolute high and water doesn't ice at the poles.
A cliff – or a cutting – holds a lifetime of fossils.
Look at its rhythmic packages of sediment.
Track its tectonic upheavals into anticline:
church, ark, *structure*. Encounter it at Ventnor
or Eastbourne or in the Aughrimderg borehole.
Study the blocks of its consonants, its breathy vowel.
Watch dark fricatives spark in the lyric ground.

Bloodstone Copse

It has taken coming here to start
going back. I skirt the road to reach
this little coppice, refuge for earthstars,

toothwort, violets. I walk and watch
the unmarked fields unfold as wood inclines
to valley, and valley shades to down, and each

returns me to another landscape: mine.
This place is ringed in chalk as if to note
its own significance. The water underlines

itself in red – albeit with algal blooms and not,
as locals have it, blood-blotched stones,
though the difference is too slight to notice:

the Danes may well have slain the Saxons
here. I wear Twyford as a wound.
My mouth is raw. I am open for salvation.

Bourne

I lived as a child in Chandler's Ford,
whose name comes from a farmstead
near a fording point. We'd lose ourselves

at The Lakes, totally absorbed in water, diverted
by engineering dams and navigations,
knee-deep in smelly reddish mud.

Which is a tributary to –

Summer walks along the River Itchen
with our pastel-coloured fishing nets dangling
in the clean bright water.

Once we caught a white-clawed crayfish
and rushed it back to show the adults
in an empty plastic ice-cream tub.

Which is a tributary to –

1st Otterbourne Brownies: Monday evenings
in the dusty Village Hall dancing
round a heavy wooden toadstool.

I earned my Writer Badge after a tussle
over whether 'teasel' was a word.
I knew it was: I'd seen them by the river.

Which is a tributary to –

My mother had her womb cut out
in Winchester Hospital.

When we went to visit
she was whiter than a feeling.

Which is a tributary to –

Sunday mornings helping at the children's home
across the water meadows in St Cross.

The kids would cling to you like riverweed.

Which is a tributary to –

Working in the children's section of Winchester Library.
I travelled up by rail every weekday from Southampton.

Which is a tributary to –

I saw the river from the rattling train
through the window you pulled down

to reach for the handle at the station
where you wanted to alight –

the riverweed trailing in impeccable currents,
the impossible clarity of water.

And beyond it I saw
the end of a green hill turned white.

Desire Lines

take this Late Bronze Age trackway of close-packed flint and chalk within a shallow terrace

its horizontal base cut into the natural rock, its metalled surface heavily worn

or this early Roman trackway crossing the lynchets over to the west or

this *series of interconnecting hollow-ways, known locally as the Dongas* –

landscape of passage, drove-route, gallops –

take this, take this, take this

Barrow

Drive through the cutting in your metal avatar –
high above your lone dark line spins
memory's bright ring of bones.

I'm not sure where I am. In here it's dark
despite this thin white sheet they've used to line
my bed-box, and my amber beads. The metal
of the sides is some new-fangled thing, its ring
quite different from bronze, or stone. Old bones
can tell you what you didn't know. Cut

to that time not long ago when they cut
through the flint rubble into the dark
where I'd crouched for aeons. Light tickled my bones
like their little brushes. A whole line
of us they dug up, out of our ring-
ditch, sealing the finish of the dawn of metal.

But what a dawn! Women rowed metal
along the coast in a wooden cutter:
tin from Cornwall, which didn't so much ring
as cry, and copper from Kerry; leaving the dark
behind them forever, drawing a line
under the future. They felt it in their bones.

I always loved to watch the bonfires:
flesh melting in flame, the flash of metal
trinkets on the skin, the smell of burning linen
mingling with the onion couch grass we'd cut
to use as tinder then pile on the pyre in the dark
before we'd gather round the dead one in a ring.

As a girl, I helped the women cut the clearing
in the wood. We worked our fingers to the bone
hacking back the ash and thorn, opening the dark.
That kind of toil really puts you on your mettle,
and don't get me started on cutting
the ring-ditch, but you had to toe the line.

Tales of our foremothers were passed down the line –
'the sizzle of their alchemy' – but didn't ring
true. It took my grandmother to cut
to the chase, put flesh on the bones,
tell how they'd crush the country rock – the *metal* –
conjure liquid amber from the dark.

The Finds

i.

WORKED-BONE BELT-HOOK FRAGMENT

parallel grooves
on outer curved surface

pass for

parallel grooves
on outer curved surface

Woodsmoke

Sit in the open round
          fires in the evening
               blackened
kettles hissing hanging
        from an iron tripod

Smell it clinging
       thick inside your hair
            it blows you back
off-centre
               somewhere earlier and farther
where bodies worked
       fetched wood and dried it
chopped –
        beyond electricity
past the quick
       of heat and light
           sucked
through skin and into us

Sit in woodsmoke as the wind shifts
          it will make you smart

ii.

CERAMIC BUILDING MATERIAL

No *antefix*, that's true, with or without vine leaves and grapes or a Gorgon's head, but eight *tegulae*, six *imbrices* (the bits and pieces of their ridge-and-furrowed roofs) and twelve brick fragments – possibly from *besales*, which supported the floor

above the hollow of a hypocaust, stacked in pillars. I like to think of the Romans nestled in their *settlement involving substantial buildings* in the first century near the toe of Twyford Down looking over at St Catherine's Hill

not knowing, for how could they, that what would come careering through two thousand years later would be the offspring of their own invention. I'm glad to know about their houses, though.

Camp

I remember the cold. We'd huddle round the burner
in the central bender; the metal flue meandered up and out.

We wore a lot of green, that colour of the patina on copper.
I had a bright blue cagoule and tried to dye it black in the bath
at home to make it duller.

We cooked frazers, short for self-raisers, from flour, water,
salt, and a little spice. We'd flatten the dough with our hands,
press it into rounds.

This sometimes led to Donga Belly, so our shit turned yellow
and smelled of rotten eggs.

iii.

POSSIBLY A SMALL TUBULAR GOAD –

penannular in cross-section, broken
projection, collar formed from iron strip
– similar to one from Vindolanda –
but note *A note concerning 'ox goads'* buried
in a report, how traces of ink were noticed
at the foot of the shaft of one example,
how another has some of the wood
still surviving – hollowed out to form
a capillary running through its centre –
and, noting that desire is constructed
almost entirely of absence, how this
in itself is a stimulus or spur, know that
though no wooden shaft is present here, if
on a replica used by the author the channel-
like feature was found to act very well
in drawing ink up, this is almost certainly
a nib.

Where the Wild Things Are

Winchester, Wednesday 9 December 1992

I am working in the library reshelving books.
On a hill, a mile away, all hell is breaking loose.
I skulk in the aisles of the children's section
sticking missing picture labels onto spines:
white butterflies fluttering over grassland,
serious owls in the blue of night, rabbits
with bobtails angled cheekily at borrowers.
I decide to display *The Very Hungry Caterpillar*
then, on a whim, *The Tiger Who Came to Tea*.
I have a go on the laminator; the acrid taste
of melting plastic film hangs in the carrels.
I'll tackle minor book repairs tomorrow.

Winchester, Thursday 10 December 1992

I've hardly slept and smell of woodsmoke.
All our books are broken
and I have no heart for mending.
How can I replace these torn end sheets?
Flyleaves have been ripped from pastedowns.
Folded signatures have come unsewn.
Joints are bent forever out of kilter.
Beaded headbands flap, detached.
I am not equipped to glue spines back.
I seek out Maurice Sendak's book –
those yellow eyes and terrible teeth –
before I can start to write what I have seen.

The Ballad of Yellow Wednesday

after Federico García Lorca

Wednesday 9 December 1992

Black gape the digger buckets.
The tyres tread black.
The yellow plastic jackets
are spattered with diesel.
These men don't cry: their skulls
are leaden as their hard hats.
With yellow plastic souls
they have come for their road.
Humpbacked and brutal,
they drive through the dark.
Under silent black rubber
the trembling chalk.
They cut where they want to cut,
conceal in their minds
a ghostly cosmology
of petrol-blue lines.

Oh Dongas camp!
with your tarpaulin benders,
garlic planted by moonlight,
and sloe-reddened gin.
Oh Dongas camp!
Whoever saw you could forget?
Camp of comfrey and sadness,
hold high your sage sticks!

At nightfall the night
falls pitch-black as bitumen.
The Dongas in their benders
lash hazel into pentacles.
A single nightwatchwoman
runs from tent to tent.
'Aruga! Aruga!'
she sounds the alarm.
Even the wind
has got wind of the danger
as tar-black night turns
to tremulous dawn.

Oh Dongas camp!
with your tarpaulin benders,
cover your burners,
here comes the DoT.
Oh Dongas camp!
Whoever saw you could forget?
May your trackways forever
comb the unparted hill.

Two by two they advance
on the wakening Dongas.
A murmur of flowers
infringes their pockets.
Two by two they advance,
this PVC army. The sky
blazes with fluorescence:
a yellow plastic dawn.

For centuries footpaths
have furrowed the hill.
Now eighty hired guards
move in to remove them.
The cycle of nature
creaks to a standstill.
Clustered bellflowers
cloak themselves in winter.
Chalkhill blue butterflies
weep as they scatter.
Turf is trampled by Hard Hats
then ripped up by bulldozers,
but the young Donga women
don't flee through the shadows.
They lie under the earthmovers,
a crock of rare coins.
Those sinister jackets
climb the steep slopes
leaving coils of razor wire
whirling in their wakes.

In the middle of the bedlam
the tribe gathers round
a Donga girl throttled
by the hood of her anorak.
Dull thwacks and thuds
resound through the day.
The heads of Donga men split
under boot, under fist.
But the DoT drives on,

heaping trees into bonfires.
Green imaginations
burn with the sycamores.
One of the tribe slumps
groaning by her bender,
her neck ligaments torn,
her arm in a sling.
Other women keep running
in front of the machines,
their beaded hair trailing
through pulverised chalk.
With all of its flints
lined up in the ground,
the Down rocks its shoulders
in a long sweep of stone.

Oh Dongas camp!
Now the guards are fenced in
by a silent ring of wire
it is time for dancing!

The Tofu Love Frogs
bring fiddles and drums,
come looking for the Dongas
to see if they can find them.
One girl wears a flower
on the knee of her trousers,
scraps of cloth in her hair,
and a necklace of triangles.
Workers huddle round braziers

under arc light glare
as earth's dark shutters
close over the moon.
The eclipse, half-elapsed,
spawns a frenzy of dancing.
With banners and lanterns
the tribe tramples the wire.
Their twisting hips mirror
the turbulent day.
Laughter and weeping
echoes through Winchester.

Oh Dongas camp!
Whoever saw you could forget?
Your gullies furrow my brow.
A maze of moon and chalk.

iv.

LOOMWEIGHT

*One degraded chalk weight, [...] pear-shaped form
and countersunk perforation towards one end*

They blocked the footpath over the downs with the razor wire of their compound, and a metal gate. We pulled it off its hinges; it was wrestled back and forth in a kind of tug-of-war. Without a gate, they blocked the path by linking their yellow arms. We went round them and over the fence by laying bits of old carpet over the barbs. We'd run in as far as we could, then lie down on the footpath till they carried or dragged us back out. Then we'd do it again. I remember lying on the soft grass and being picked up by two security guards, one taking both my arms and one both my legs. I made myself as heavy as I could, letting my body hang down in an arc. I was pleased that I was tall and heavy and hard to shift. Direct action is a physical thing. It
is
of the
body.

v.

BUCKET URN

with row of bosses fairly well down the body;
sometimes linked by fingertip-impressed cordon

Nervous as animals, short-back-and-sided,
recruited off the dole on Youth Training
Schemes, or ex-soldiers cursing the day
they were sent to be muddied high on a hill
on a grey winter morning, linking arms
at the elbow in waterproof jackets – yellow,
with a shining belt around each girth &
a shining bib strap across each chest
& over both shoulders, like braces –
hard-hatted men brawling for wages,
manhandling women, pressure-pointing
their necks: pressing in under each ear
with leather-covered fingertips
to shut off oxygen to the head.

vi.

FOURTEEN AMBER BEADS (CHOKER)

The only certain grave goods from the barrow are 14 amber beads from a single inhumation.

The bulldozers gleamed in the early morning sunshine, the chalk a foil for their yellow. Becca locked herself on by the neck underneath one of them, between the front wheels, with a black D-lock – the kind you'd use to lock up your bike outside the post office. I locked myself on to the footplate. Some workers arrived, then the police. They politely asked us to unlock ourselves; we politely declined. The sun rose a little higher and the sky turned from pink to blue above the white chalk. We sat locked by the neck to the yellow machine. The men ambled around

trying to decide what to do. What they did was unscrew, bolt by bolt, the entire top section of the chassis – like an enormous yellow cheese grater. They asked me to stand while they supported the frame at all four corners. I stood in the hole in the middle of this heavy piece of metal, still attached by the neck, as the men edged me and my outsize necklace to the side of the worksite where they hacksawed my D-lock off. Becca cheered and laughed as she stayed fixed under the bulldozer. The men ambled around a bit more, wondering what on earth to do about her.

vii.

BRONZE BROOCH WITH MOCK SPRING

&

the earthmovers flying down the hill with their buckets raised high

(each full of chalk)

& at the foot of the hill the buckets tipping forwards

& angling downwards

& mass after mass of crumbling white chalk being dumped in the river

& white water splashing up

& the white swans swimming there taking to the air

Crosses

Sunday 7 February 1993

That cold day we walked on opened chalk.
We marched in procession up the cutting
each carrying a wooden cross painted black

with, on a white panel, in wobbly writing,
the name of a plant or animal or bird
whose habitat the road was obliterating.

The labels of the species are blurred.
In the distance, a line of cars – the metal
river out of which we have emerged.

We're dressed in black, not red for battle:
not so much a protest as a wake.
But take a look again, see how little

of the chalk has yet been cut away –
most of the hill is still intact,
not fully hollowed for the motorway.

Lines of flint stick out of the surface, packed
in heavy, rounded clumps, like cannonballs
or wayside cairns. I follow them back

to that photo from the Crimean War,
or rather to that pair of photos.
There are two versions, one transformed

by altering the landscape that was photographed
by placing cannonballs along a road
to underline the symbol of the photo.

Look at its title, *Valley of the Shadow*
of Death, which carries me back to the flora
and fauna on the crosses that we made:

ROCK-ROSE I can easily remember
because it's the one I was holding
and *COOT, RUFF, SISKIN, REED WARBLER,*

as later, during the court proceedings,
in an act of divine comedy,
the Department of Transport resorted to calling

a handful of protesters after the names
of the species scribbled on their crosses,
so these live on – in both memory

and dog-eared press cuttings – as aliases.
Though we walk through the valley of shadows,
birds still sing in other places.

Human Chain

after Seamus Heaney

Sunday 7 March 1993

Looking at the blocks of chalk passed hand to hand
by the protesters – silhouettes of black
against the white and desecrated land,

like Lowry's workers near a factory
or a thinning stand of trees –
each caught in the act of putting something back –

how insignificant the cars and lorries
in the background are, how clear and strong
the image of people aligning is –

still moving to rebuild the Down.
We are only ever passing through.
We are supposed to pass this on.

Morning Hills, with Dragon

Wednesday 28 April 1993

We started off at a quick pace, the Prefects walking on the road,
the rest on the footpath, all of us dressed 'up to Books'

Her yellow sunflower eyes

on we went, the small College boys at a sharp trot to keep up
with the long strides of the bigger ones in front

Her terrible teeth

round the corner of Warden's garden, on past Commoner's Field
and Domum tree, over the three stepping-stiles and up the steep ascent
of St Catherine's Hill

Green spirals on her long white flank

and on the slope to the west of the maze, the calling of names,
followed by prayers

Purple scales hanging

forgive us our trespasses, as we forgive those who trespass against us

Her yellow sunflower eyes

by and by the voices of three Juniors warned that it was time to go 'on'

Her terrible teeth

two of them made the circuit of 'Trench'; the other crossed the summit of Hills

Green spirals on her long white flank

then at a signal from the Prefect of Hall below

Purple scales hanging

we rushed down to Tunbridge and were marshalled on our way home

Her yellow sunflower eyes

Her terrible teeth

Green spirals on her long white flank

Purple scales hanging

Claw

I am looking it up in the dictionary. A clutch of protesters are looking out
at the landscape beyond. The sky is white, whiter than the chalk below
the digger bucket on which they stand. I read: earth in very fine particles,
tenacious and impervious. But the earth has slipped and my index finger
with it. This is the primary definition of *clay*.

I go back: the hooked nail of a mammal, bird or reptile, or
the creature's foot with a number of such nails; also to scratch,
scrape, seize; to make an arm movement with the fingers bent.
Related to cleave[2]: to stick or adhere, to unite, but not to cleave[1]:
to divide or split, to cut through, to crack.

At the instant of the shutter click, the claw is not
cutting through anything. Nothing cracks.
A handful of people have stilled the machine.
They stick together; they are united.
This way is etymology embodied.

The arm of the digger is an arm –
it has a wrist and elbow. The eight-foot
forearm splits into radius and ulna;
dark sinews bind the joints. The bucket
is big enough to hold two men:

behind their calves
its nails; beneath
their feet
a scar

—

Toll

Saturday 22 May 1993

We pulled away the razor wire, pushed the fencing
flat, and we were in, then up, then on, all
two hundred of us, swarming above the valley
on the girders of their Bailey bridge.
All night we banged out rhythms with whatever tools
we had to hand: we made the metal sing,
brought forth a chime, a knell, a toll,
a resounding reverberation, a peal;
with measured strokes we struck the bracing
frames as if they'd been cast from bell metal.
From beneath our huddled silhouettes, all
across the landscape you could hear the bridge
finding the colour of its voice, rejoicing.
The toll rings out across the valley still.

Action File 36

How do we respond to something
that we've lost: a love, a hill, a file?
Faced with spaces we try to fill
them in to bring the lost thing back.

We begin, do we not, by describing
what's mislaid or gone forever:
in this case, a bundle of paper,
A3, without a sturdy front or back.

Joined at the edges with a claw.
Inside, several pictures to a page,
each a thumbnail of a photograph
in grainy shades of grey and black.

My file was one of seventy-seven,
one for each of us: an individual
record of our protest actions,
a private gallery of what we did.

Delivered in the black of night
by jaunty men in flashy cars,
door-stepping us at home,
making sure they caught us in.

They gave each file a number.
We printed these on A4 paper
and pinned them to our fronts
before we crossed the fence.

We can enter through an image
or a form: here, a set of images,
now lost, of people in a landscape,
the form of which is also lost.

We could look the key words up:
file – a line of soldiers, to bring
before a court, an instrument
with sharp-edged furrows.

We might try to enter through
a glossary, but the legal papers
being these days also largely lost
frees us up to say things simply.

What I remember of my file is
lots of pictures of me standing
near diggers. The chalk always
appeared grey, but it was white.

I remember how anxious
I looked: my fingers bent,
the fingertips of one hand
worrying those of the other.

In the end don't we merely
put ourselves back in
the picture – centre frame –
as in any proper elegy.

Injunction

Sunday 4 July 1993

Over under through?
I cannot remember how

we crossed the fence
but there was dancing

on the other side
and we were joined

Statement

High Court, London, Friday 23 July 1993

'My Lord, I would like to explain why I took the decision to defy the High Court Injunction of 2nd July, which forbids me from walking on what was once Twyford Down. My protest is not aimed at you, My Lord, and I have no desire to seem disobedient in the eyes of the Court. My protest is against the Department of Transport. It is only because they have chosen to employ heavy-handed legal action to try to stifle our protest that I now find myself in conflict with the Court.

I grew up a few miles from Twyford Down and walked over its beautiful rolling slopes on many occasions. Now Twyford Down is a gaping chasm and the Itchen Valley at its foot has an enormous embankment stretching across it. By this process of turning hills into valleys and valleys into hills, the Department of Transport is levelling our nation's heritage and history. Twyford Down encapsulated 100 million years of geological history and 4,000 years of human history. I cannot consent to the wilful annihilation of such an immense swathe of our heritage by an ephemeral government. To have ceased protesting in the face of this desecration would have meant giving that consent.

But I have an even more serious reason for defying the injunction and continuing my protest. The levelling of the landscape that I have witnessed at Twyford Down is not a special case. The Department of Transport intends, through its road-building programme, to repeat the process at more than 1000 other protected heritage sites and green spaces. It seeks to radically alter the topography of this land, to destroy 160 Sites of Special Scientific Interest, 800 Scheduled Ancient Monuments, 12 Areas of Outstanding Natural Beauty and two National Parks. In short, the DoT is seeking to remove idiosyncrasy from the landscape, to make one place in Britain just like any other by levelling it off and covering it in tarmac.

I cannot sit back and let this happen. The continuing protest at Twyford Down is helping to save these threatened sites. Already the proposed road through Lugg Meadows Site of Special Scientific Interest in Herefordshire has been dropped on environmental grounds and, of course, we have recently celebrated the victory at Oxleas Woods. The wonderful news that this beautiful tract of ancient woodland is to be spared the bulldozer came just a couple of days after the defiance of the injunction at Twyford Down. It has been widely acknowledged, even, indirectly, by that fulcrum of the road lobby, the British Road Federation itself, that our continuing protests at Twyford Down played a significant role in the reprieve of Oxleas Woods.

Sustaining the protest at Twyford Down has, then, begun to make a difference to the preservation of the beauty spots and historic past of Britain. It is unfortunate that we have had to come into conflict with the law to achieve this, for, as I said, there is no quarrel with the law. Simon Hughes MP said, "There is a time and place for peaceful law-breaking, as, on occasion, it is necessary for right to prevail". In this case "right" means an intact Britain. It means a Britain which will survive this Government with some of its history left and with some of its green fields remaining. I cannot stand idly by whilst the Department of Transport bulldozes through our countryside – scouring out a huge cutting through Lympne Scarp in Kent or building an embankment the height of a telegraph pole across water meadows in sight of Salisbury cathedral. This is not progress, it is madness and I cannot just sit back and watch.'

Sentence

Mr Justice Alliott, High Court, London, Friday 23 July 1993

'Nothing is more saddening than when a judge is faced with the inevitable task of passing prison sentences on people who are fundamentally decent and motivated by a concern which to them overrides everything else.

You have been quick to snatch the martyr's crown and you may find it uncomfortable headgear.'

Holloway Letters
(The Martyr's Crown)

for Becca Lush

*holloway – lane or path that has been grooved down
into the landscape due to the erosive power of,
variously, feet, wheels and rainwater*

[Correspondence I]

I've done my time learning how to write back.
I'm rereading what's inside these two fat packets
after twenty-five years: my half of the letters
– we split them in two when they let us out –
two hundred-odd assorted envelopes
addressed to Prisoner TV3514
or 3515, or both, HMP Holloway,

from close and distant family, campaigners,
former colleagues at the library,
offices of politicians, orienteers,
school friends, ex-boyfriends, my old headmaster,
colleagues of ex-boyfriends, former housemates,
the lads in Pentonville, folk up trees in Newcastle,
and loads of people we didn't know at all.

[Correspondence II]

And loads of people we didn't know at all,
who write: 'It's bloody madness!' 'Good for you!'
'We are all indebted to you all'
or 'I was really shocked' or simply 'Thank you.'
I'm a bit embarrassed by their gushing
– 'your stand', 'your bravery' – but also very touched.
There's wisdom here, too, in snippets: 'They can cut
down all the flowers but they cannot stop the spring.'

And look! A letter from my Great Aunt Marjorie:
'We all went through a war to keep U. K.
a lovely country, we must keep it green and free.'
And something else I'd forgotten till today:
amid the homespun philosophy and memories,
pictures of the outdoors, above all, trees.

[Woods]

Pictures of the outdoors, above all, trees,
newly released from their paper sleeves,
expand to fill this narrow room: *Springtime
in the Forest of Dean*; *View from Rungaroon,
with old tree covered in epiphytes in foreground*;
Autumn, Parkland Walk; *Bluebell Wood, England*;
drawings of *Glen Feardar* and *Glen Tanar*.

The beauty of the land let loose in here,
displayed in jumbled clusters on the floor.
My favourite is *Cycle Path in Rail Tunnel
on Westside of Dartmoor near Clearbrook* –
a dark entrance in a mossy glade –
No. 1 in a Series of 6.
The possibilities contained in this!

[Inspection of One's Person]

The possibilities contained in this
or any prison van en route to any prison.
We were escorted from the court by two tipstaffs:
a staff tipped with metal; an officer who carries it.
The van had velvet seats, but bars across the windows.
On arrival, we were weighed and measured by a nurse,
asked about our mental state, then strip-searched

– the bit I'd dreaded, but it was nothing more
than taking off my top, lifting under my bra
and pulling down my trousers. They confiscated
most of the stuff I'd brought in – hair ties,
toothpaste – sent me to sit with the other new inmates,
armed with a nightie and a zip-lock bag of toiletries.
You learn not to ask 'What are you in for?'

[What She Was In For]

You learn not to ask 'What are you in for?'
but what she was in for was parking on the road
outside her house to get her kids inside
before she'd find a space to leave the car.
And what she was in for was passport fraud:
she'd made it here over several seas,
her dignity locked in a single plait.

And what she was in for was possession.
And what she was in for was being poor,
unable to pay for her TV licence.
And what she was in for was her son,
doing time for *his* non-payment of a fine.
She'll tell you soon enough, in passing.
It's the one thing you should never ask.

[Bird]

It's the one thing you should never ask,
besides 'Please could you turn your radio off?'
It's on 3pm to midnight without a break,
and LOUD. I try asking her to turn it down.
It's not turned up, she says, she's doing
a long sentence and it's the only thing
that is keeping her sane. It's driving
me mad, I say, and I can't get out.

If I'd known back then about St Kevin,
I might have had a go at sticking my arm
out the window, turned my palm to heaven,
and waited till a blackbird chanced to nest.
It's not that the pain would have brought me rest,
but that we hold small hopes in our own hands.

[Wasted]

But that we hold small hopes in our own hands,
or under our pillows. She'd save the little capsules –
half eggshell blue, half oxblood red – till Friday
for her hit, casual as anything, though her nagging
every evening when the drugs trolley glided
along the corridor rather undermined her cool:
'Go on, get me some, go on, go on.'

Or she'd wait for visiting time and 'crotch it' –
reach up inside the small frayed hole
between her thighs – or swallow then retch
the stuff up later in a mess of Mars bar.
But mostly she was waiting for her Discharge Grant.
Our cellmate banged her head against the wall;
you couldn't say anything to comfort her at all.

[Fitted]

You couldn't say anything to comfort her at all.
She got more and more obsessive
about food and exercise and cleanliness
and tidiness and people stealing things.
The doctor said she might be 'shipped out'
to another prison, so she starved herself:
too thin and she wouldn't be 'fitted'.

She wanted to go to C4, where she had a friend.
Another cellmate had different plans.
To get back to the medical block
she had to produce a bottleful of diarrhoea
so spent the morning giving herself an enema
with a washing-up-liquid bottle full of water.
Everybody was on the go.

[Wing]

Everybody was on the go.
The moment that they let her out
Becca would turn cartwheels up and down
the wing: she'd bend at the waist,
reach down with her hands, drive the back leg
over her head, land with the kick leg,
push with her hands, bring the other foot
down, and stand. Hand, hand, foot, foot.

Momentum was important, and while the sun
on her regal purple T-shirt rose and set
and rose again as she sprang sure-footed
on the shiny floor, the fingers of each hand
turned into wingtip, though she stayed rooted,
like the cork oak, in a circle of herself.

[Canerow]

Like the cork oak, in a circle of herself,
each full-grown woman would turn a little girlish
at the prospect of a proper hairdo.

Sitting in lines of three or four, or pairs,
we'd plait each other's hair in tight, flat rows –

part a section to get things started,
make stitch braids out of the strands,
adding in hair from the row below.

We dreamed in parallel:
of fields double dug, rough-hoed by the tiller
then ploughed into kick-waves of keels and furrows …

We'd reach the nape and keep on plaiting,
secure each end with a snap bead, bolo tip or barrette,
our loose braids mirrored as a shoal of minnows.

[Wild]

Our loose braids mirrored as a shoal of minnows,
we'd go to 'Education' in the library
and browse through *De Profundis*
or *The Ballad of Reading Gaol*. You could chat
to Annette Tibbles: in for years for conspiracy
to free caged rabbits, so she got a job
shelving novels and looked after the cats.

Dear Annette, thank you for the Marmite
and that amazing information about
police surveillance tactics. I hope
you are out now, that you live on a farm
somewhere quiet with as many animals
as you care to love, rear, feed,
and as many books as you care to read.

[Shares]

And as many books as you care to read
would not be enough to haggle for a lighter,
which, after tobacco, tops the hierarchy
of tradable prison commodities.
You'd hear tales of a two-day barter:
the swapping of a sweatshirt for a quarter
of a matchstick, split along its length.

I was more than happy to peddle hair gel
for chocolate to eke out the portions
dished up in the small dining hall
on a tray filled with hollows –
supper at four then you'd starve till morning.
We swapped a bit of this for a bit of that,
though some would give anything to exchange futures.

[Home]

Though some would give anything to exchange futures,
we were content in our new, shared cell.
We shunted our metal beds into an 'L'
and pinned up a cutting of the cutting
from the *Guardian* to make it more homely.
We learnt that letters out must be unsealed;
that letters in could be collected at 11.30;
that we got a lot more letters than anyone else.

Letters matter. Once, before our appeal,
I was woken by a face through the grille:
'You're on production.' It disturbed the whole dorm.
In the middle of the night, I got up and packed
and everyone started writing letters home.
I've done my time learning how to write back.

Appeal

Court of Appeal, London, Thursday 29 July 1993

'Never again must the sickening crunch of digger bucket on chalk be heard in this land simply for the sake of building roads that lead nowhere. The Department of Transport must be stopped in its tracks. I will keep protesting as long as that takes.'

Judgement

Lord Justice Hoffman, Court of Appeal, London, Thursday 29 July 1993

'I respect the opinions of the appellants. They are frank, straightforward and sincere young women and there is nothing irrational about their conscientiously held views on the need to preserve the countryside. Furthermore, civil disobedience on grounds of conscience is an honourable tradition in this country and those who take part in it may in the end be vindicated by history.'

Native Species

after Michael Longley

Fraggle, Alex, Howie, Heather, Rosie, Sam,
and nameless others I have missed,
I will name for you once more the wild flowers
you lived among: Thyme, Rock-rose, Cowslip,
Clustered Bellflower, Hairy Violet, Fairy Flax,
Kidney Vetch, Horseshoe Vetch, Salad Burnet,
Frog Orchid, Bastard Toadflax, Hemp Agrimony,
Devil's-bit Scabious, Fleabane, Autumn Lady's Tresses.

Motorway

There's no unbroken arc of chalk,
a curve of sky across its back,
nor grasses stippling the space between.

It is wanting swans beneath its foot,
and sycamore, and hawthorn.
There's nothing in the way of flowers.

There are no bodies curled in pits,
no disarticulated bone, nor any wrist
still crossed behind.

The place is bare of amber beads,
quernstones, loomweights, brooches.
Worked bone is long fragmented.

There are no nights
when the only noise is night
and hill.

What there is is whiteness rubbing off
on cuffs of afternoons as we pass
blocks of chalk from grasp to grasp

along the filling line.

Fathom

This Solid and Drift Geology Map
laid out on the kitchen table
has reminded me all week
of the top-right corner of a painting
by Jackson Pollock in which a lozenge
of the deepest colour is cupped
by a moon of pale green.
The upper layers comprise poured
lines of black. A section of river
cuts through the work in orange
and yellow. The paint enfolds
an assortment of detritus: butts
of cigarettes, and coins, and keys.

As for the map, I am only concerned
with its south-east corner: Winchester.
The rocks look like an eye.
Something is cutting through
the sclera, not the road I feared
and would wake sweating over,
but the river – its alluvium
the width of a finger, a channel
as broad as a stem. I can measure
its reach with my arms outstretched.
The tufa is silty with calcareous nodules.
Raised hummocks signal the winter's level.
A leaf of strata waves from the gravels.

Ground Truth

Where are the songs of Spring? Ay, where are they?
                                                    – Keats

Saturday 9 December 2017

Dawn

A moon cut in half – lengthways – hangs
above the engines of the plane
and cloud-down lies soft under our wings
like the dorsal feathers of a swan.
Out of the deep blue valleys of the night,
dawn is happening. The sky is lightening –
the orange-pink of morning gathers over
the horizon. The day is turning yellow,
and I am heading towards it.
                                        A half-moon.
I could hardly have dreamt of such a symbol:
the white part like a hill of chalk, wheeled
on its axis far enough to change the world.
Beneath the cloud, now patching into mackerel,
the segregated fields are becoming visible:
each a different shade of white outlined in black.
Where are we now? It's hard to get your bearings.
A Red Funnel Ferry from the Isle of Wight –
that must be Southampton Water.

Morning

A bright clear day. A blessing.
The train waits for ages at Eastleigh.
Two vapour trails make an X in the sky,
like that demo before election day.
We are still being held here. Yellow
metal gantries remind me of home.
And we're off. First glimpses of the Itchen
curving lazily through water meadows,
then, as we draw near to Shawford, swans! –
calm in the sun and the water glinting.
I'm grateful for the halt, to still us –
me – before we pass ... what? This train
doesn't rattle, but the heating hums.
PLEASE KEEP BEHIND THE YELLOW LINE
UNTIL THE TRAIN HAS STOPPED.
And now we pull away ...
                                        First sight.
How can they bear it, those who live here still?
It has very much greened over – the scar
is not bright white. An old wound healing?

Town

The handsome station clock still marking
time, then *Lily and the Little Snow Bear*
at the Theatre Royal. I almost trip over
a plaque explaining how the County Gaol
was turned into the library – my own journey

in reverse. Heading down the high street
everything is proto-Christmas: 'The holly
and the ivy, when they are both full grown,
of all the trees that are in the wood, the holly
bears the crown' pumped out in cool soft 'o's
by the Salvation Army band. The Buttercross –
that focus for dissent across the years –
is decked out in blue flags with yellow stars:
Exit from Brexit! This takes me back
to February '93 when Becca
and I would shiver behind a rickety
pasting table gathering signatures
for our petition to the European Commission.
Plus ça change?
                    Then a sharp right turn
into the cathedral grounds past buskers
vying for attention: the university bunch
with their bobble hats, battered guitars
and youthful voices are winning out
when judged by any yardstick – volume,
exuberance, general stopping value –
over a crew dressed up like characters
from Dickens, who are not even bothering
to sing until the students stop,
                              and on, on …
to the river, but not before I run the gauntlet
of the Christmas market with its stained-wood sheds,
pyramids of red-rimmed barrel-ends
and a practically full-scale ice rink.

The revellers are guided through the tinsel
by an over-ambitious one-way system.
I cannot wait to leave. I find an exit
between walls of flint and brick: 'Rejoice!
Rejoice!' fades into the distance ...

Soon the *Caring for Winchester's Heritage* signs
recede and I reach the Abbey Gardens,
my first sight of riverweed in twenty-odd years.
*There are only around 200 chalk rivers
in the world and more than three quarters
of them are found in England,* I'm informed,
amid the sound of water plunging under the pillars
of the River Cottage Canteen, where mallards
comically upend themselves to feed.
Their heads are even greener than the weed.

... And on to find the river proper. A sign
says *South Downs Way.* That's new. Another
tells of historical diversions, splittings
of the channel to lessen flooding risk,
and how in medieval times the river
was twice as wide as it is today. We live
in a living landscape. We change it.
Then ... Swans! Two, so far, eating.
I'm disorientated. I brought a map,
but haven't used it. Is that Arethusa's Clump?

Noon

I choose to ignore the tourist path
up St Catherine's Hill, and seek the way
we always went: up Plague Pits Valley.
Thick-trunked beech trees bear witness to the past.
I keep walking. Steep chalk slopes to my left,
the Itchen Navigation to my right.
And suddenly: *THIS MILEPOST*
IS SITUATED 26½ MILES
FROM NEWBURY AND WAS ORIGINALLY
PLACED ALONGSIDE THE FORMER DIDCOT, NEWBURY
AND SOUTHAMPTON RAILWAY UP THE BANK.
All the while the constant sound of traffic
in the distance; now and then a passing train.
Across the water meadows the squat tower
of St Cross corroborates what has come and gone.
The hum of traffic is growing louder now:
a low rumble punctuated by horns.
(I remember, as I sit down
for a bit, one protester who drank
a flask of stagnant water from the canal
and had to have his stomach pumped.)
Not much here in the way of birds, but,
off and on, a great tit. Ok, ok …

Twyford Down

Its name airbrushed out of the landscape.
No sign heralds your arrival.

Instead, a flashy information board
peddles nature propaganda: pastel-coloured
naïve art depicting rough hawkbit,
kidney vetch, small blue, marbled white,
pyramidal orchid, eyebright,
quaking grass. All around us, the noise
of cars and lorries. Waves of cars and lorries.
Folds. The hum the hum the hum the hum.
It has taken going back to stop coming
here, in nightmare and in memory.
Not a soul in this valley today but me.
They've all been shuttled up St Catherine's Hill.
The sun is low over the Down, or its shell.

Then: a single blackbird, a clump
of brambles. Many clumps of brambles.
And now the roar. From the footbridge over
the motorway where the Dongas were –
three lines of traffic in each direction,
a grass-covered central reservation,
and a greyish cutting with the beds
of chalk and flint still visible beneath
the scree. *Soft estate*, my arse.
There are no rabbits skipping in this cutting,
no butterflies aflutter, just cars and cars
and cars and cars and lorries rushing –
where? And an electronic road sign:
TO J4 (M27) 7 MINS
in orange letters on black, and a blue one:

M3 Southampton 11. Hardware. Nothing
soft here now. This is no place
to linger.

On the other side of the motorway,
by what is left of one end of one Donga,
a sign reads *Please treat this sensitive area
with respect,* the logo of Winchester College
in the bottom right-hand corner.
Then, scared off course by a fearsome ram,
I find our stone! The slab that Simon
carved, which we dragged up here with ropes
and rollers, fallen over now – a proper
monument. *THIS LAND WAS
RAVAGED BY,* and then a list, all men
except for one: M. Thatcher. In the fence
between it and the motorway,
two strands of wire hung with ribbons –
in memoriam – whites and greens
and blues and pinks and purples. One
yellow. I fear I've nothing to tie on.

And now a group of long-tailed tits
mirroring the ribbons in the wind …
I've found the page-marker-ribbon-
thingy from my old field-notebook.
It comes loose with a single tug.
I fix it to the fence, then turn
to the tail end of the last small Donga,
soft-bottomed with sphagnum as it ever was,
and prickled with a few low haws.

Dusk

I walk a little further. Traffic falls
into a mouth between the cutting faces
where the hill once dipped its toe into the river.
No hope of crossing here.
                              The sky has lost
its blue – thin layers of cloud are forming.
A pale sun fails to raise the level of the light.

Traffic noises itself into night.

viii.

SHALE SPINDLE WHORL

i.m. Ken Saro-Wiwa

I'll
hook you
& draw this out
attach a bundle of fleece
to the top & spin the shaft
I'll show you how to hold it all
the spindle will provide
the tension
we'll
circle back
to the Isle of Purbeck
pick up a slab of Kimmeridge shale
a blocky blackstone with thin white veins
foul-smelling sulphurous when burnt
once there were plans to light
the streets of Paris
with its gas
free
your right hand
& spin again hold the fleece
firmly between thumb & index finger
pulling slightly to put the twist in the yarn
work this material lightweight
yet strong enough to turn
on an Iron Age lathe
to fashion
amulets

the
discoid
cores of which
discarded on the beach
their centres   punched
with small square holes
were muddled up
with coins
so-
called
'coal money'
not to be confused
with ammonites conspicuous
in the shales near Washing Ledge
their pirouette of chambers sometimes
filled with pyrite or the original
aragonite of the shell
simply preserved
you've
done a length
it's time to wind it on
to drop the spindle break
it off the hook & tie a knot
run the thread up twist it round
hold everything in place
return the fleece &
start spinning
again

&
if it
should
accidentally
drop to join back on
your separate piece of you
spread out the fibres hold them
between finger & thumb
& spin once more
but make sure
there's
a
good
bit of tension
a lot of twists put in
so you can fully draw it out
let this object settle into the circle of itself
laminated slightly domed 30mm in diameter
with a small central perforation
as befits its age feel
the weight
of
the world
swinging further out
now as it takes a darker turn
& we are back in the flaming fields
of the Niger Delta where pipes
are spilling Ogoni oil &
you can see him
hanging

Notes

Several poems, or their titles and epigraphs, use words and phrases from the monograph *Twyford Down, Hampshire: Archaeological Investigations on the M3 Motorway from Bar End to Compton, 1990 – 93*, by K. E. Walker and D. E. Farwell (Winchester: Hampshire Field Club, 2000).

Some poems are ekphrastic responses to contemporaneous photos. Where this is the case, an image is included below.

—

'Chalk, with Flints'

The poem draws on ideas in Don Paterson's essay 'The Lyric Principle: Part 2: The Sound of Sense', *Poetry Review*, Volume 97:3, Autumn 2007.

'Bloodstone Copse'

A small wood near Sandown on the Isle of Wight. Thanks to Matt Kittay for first taking me there.

'Bourne'

Bourne – a stream, especially an intermittent one in chalk areas.

A line in this poem was inspired by the opening line of the poem 'Into the Hour' by Elizabeth Jennings: 'I have come into the hour of a white feeling.'

'Desire Lines'

Desire line – an unplanned route or path created through erosion by human or animal foot traffic, usually the shortest route between an origin and destination.

© Alex MacNaughton

'Barrow'

There was an Early-Middle Bronze Age barrow (burial mound) on Twyford Down, containing both inhumation and cremation burials. The barrow was thoroughly excavated in 1991 by Wessex Archaeology and the results recorded in the Hampshire Field Club monograph. Of the inhumed adults, 70% were female. The bone pathology suggested that the females 'were [either] engaged in higher risk activities than the males, or they were occasionally the subject of violent behaviour' and also indicated 'different work patterns for females and males, the onus possibly being on the females'. The poem is in the voice of skeleton 1110, an older mature adult female who was buried in a grave in the barrow ditch.

'Camp'

Thanks to Southampton poet Andy Jordan for suggesting we visit the Dongas camp in the autumn of 1992.

© Alex MacNaughton

'*iii*. POSSIBLY A SMALL TUBULAR GOAD –'

The poem incorporates material from *Lucerna*, Roman Finds Group Newsletter, 44 (January, 2013) and draws especially on the archaeological research of Robin Birley.

'The Ballad of Yellow Wednesday'

The poem is a version of Federico García Lorca's poem, 'Romance de la Guardia Civil Española' ('Ballad of the Spanish Civil Guard'). 'The DoT' is the Department of Transport.

'*iv*. LOOMWEIGHT'

A fuller prose account of this protest appears in my chapter 'Twyford Rising' in *Here We Stand: Women Changing the World*, ed. Helena Earnshaw and Angharad Penrhyn Jones (Dinas Powys: Honno, 2014).

'*v*. BUCKET URN'

© Alex MacNaughton

'Crosses'

The photo of the Crimean War referred to is 'Valley of the Shadow of Death' by Roger Fenton, reproduced in *Believing is Seeing (Observations on the Mysteries of Photography)* by Errol Morris (New York: Penguin, 2011). The quote is by Morris. Thanks to Tess Taylor for introducing me to the book. Thanks to Jan Carson for giving me Rebecca Solnit's wonderful book, *Wanderlust: A History of Walking* (London: Granta, 2014) which also informed this poem.

© Alex MacNaughton

'Human Chain'

© Hampshire Chronicle

'Morning Hills, with Dragon'

Morning Hills is one of the traditions of Winchester College. Each
year, the whole school ascends St. Catherine's Hill for a ceremony to
assert their historic rights of access. On 28 April 1993, the proceedings
were interrupted by the Dongas Dragon. The poem incorporates and
adapts material taken from the Winchester College website and from
*School-life at Winchester College; or, The Reminiscences of a Winchester
Junior under the Old Régime, 1835 – 40* by Robert Blachford Mans-
field (online).

'Claw'

© Alex MacNaughton

'Toll'

On the night of 22 May 1993, the Department of Transport's plan to build a Bailey bridge giving large earthmovers access to the construction site – code-named 'Operation Market Garden' – was disrupted by 'Operation Greenfly'.

© Alex MacNaughton

'Injunction'

'Holloway Letters (The Martyr's Crown)'

The epigraph is from *Landmarks* by Robert Macfarlane (London: Hamish Hamilton, 2015). On 23 July 1993, seven protesters were jailed for a month. The women were sent to Holloway Prison and the men to Pentonville Prison. We were released on the thirteenth day of our sentence. Becca Lush and I represented ourselves at an appeal hearing on 29 July.

'Motorway'

The motorway through Twyford Down opened in December 1994. By 1998 almost all of 'the biggest road-building programme since the Romans' had been cancelled.

© Steve Morgan / Alamy Stock Photo

'Fathom'

The painting referred to is *Full Fathom Five* by Jackson Pollock (1947).

'Ground Truth'

Ground truth is a term used in various fields, including the earth sciences, to refer to information provided by direct observation ('on the ground') as opposed to information derived by inference. I first came upon the concept of 'ground-truthing' in *Edgelands* by Paul Farley and Michael Symmons Roberts (London: Vintage, 2012).

Soft estate – 'natural habitats that have evolved along the borders and verges of motorways and trunk roads', Highways Agency, from *Landmarks* by Robert Macfarlane (London: Hamish Hamilton, 2015).

My walk, on the 25th anniversary of Yellow Wednesday, incidentally, followed much of the route of the daily walks taken by John Keats during his stay in Winchester in 1819, which provided inspiration for his ode 'To Autumn'.

'*viii*. SHALE SPINDLE WHORL'

The poem is dedicated to the memory of Nigerian environmental activist and writer, Ken Saro-Wiwa. He was awarded the Goldman Environmental Prize for Africa in 1995, the same year I was awarded the prize for Europe. According to the Goldman Prize website: 'Ken Saro-Wiwa led a peaceful movement for the environmental and human rights of Nigeria's Ogoni people whose oil-rich land has been exploited by multinational oil companies.' On 10 November 1995, the Nigerian government executed Saro-Wiwa by hanging – along with eight other Ogoni men.

Acknowledgements

Acknowledgements are due to the editors of the following publications, websites and presses which first published some of these poems, or earlier versions: *Banshee*, The Cambridge Writing Retreat, *Dark Mountain*, Ginkgo Prize, *Here We Stand: Women Changing the World* (Honno Press, 2014), The Lifeboat, *New Poets from the North of Ireland* (Blackstaff Press, 2016), *Out of Time: Poetry from the Climate Emergency* (Valley Press, 2021), Resurgence Poetry Prize, Seamus Heaney Centre, *Twyford Rising: Land and Resistance* (2020), *Under the Radar, Zócalo Public Square*.

'Where the Wild Things Are' was commended in the 2016 Resurgence Poetry Prize; 'Shale Spindle Whorl' was a commission by the Courtauld Institute of Art for RESFEST 18 (2018); 'Toll' won the Environmental Defenders Prize in the 2019 Ginkgo Prize for Ecopoetry.

Profound thanks to Sinéad Morrissey, Moyra Haslett, and, in memoriam, Ciaran Carson, for supervising my PhD in English at Queen's University Belfast, during which many of these poems were written. Thank you also to Ian Sansom and Garrett Carr.

I am deeply grateful to my poet-friends Moyra Donaldson, Connie Voisine, Mary Montague, and Rachael Hegarty for commenting on the full manuscript.

Many thanks, too, to Stephanie Conn, Paula Cunningham, Nancy Graham, Robin Ford, Patrick Fitzsymons, and the Queen's Writers Group for comments on individual poems.

Thank you to Leontia Flynn, Glenn Patterson, Rachel Brown, and Stephen Sexton at the Seamus Heaney Centre; also to Jeffrey Thomson, Erika Meitner, Wayne Miller, and Tess Taylor, whose Fulbright workshops inspired some of the poems. Thank you to Caroline Sumpter; and Lucy Collins at UCD.

Thank you to Mimi Khalvati for teaching me poetic form, back in the day. Also to Martin Edney, Chris Gillham, Pat Kinnersly, Steve Kirk, Sheila Llewellyn, and Julia Paul for various acts of kindness related to this book.

Thank you to the Arts Council of Northern Ireland National Lottery funds for financial support.

I would also like to warmly thank Damian Smyth and Paul Maddern for their invaluable encouragement across the years, and the Belfast writers Jan Carson, Maria McManus, Maureen Boyle, Malachi O'Doherty, and Mícheál McCann.

I am indebted to the team at Valley Press for publishing this book. Thank you to Jamie McGarry, Peter Barnfather, and my exceptional editor, Kate Simpson.

Many thanks indeed to Alex MacNaughton for permitting me to include his extraordinary photographs, and also to the *Hampshire Chronicle*.

Finally, I would like to thank my dear friends Jane Debono and Louise Finnis. Beautiful Louise, I'm so sorry you'll never get to read this.

Transport Action Network helps support people and groups press for more sustainable transport in England and Wales. This involves fighting cuts to bus services, particularly in rural areas, and opposing damaging road schemes and large unsustainable developments.

transportactionnetwork.org.uk

A36/A350
CORRIDOR
ALLIANCE

Formed after the protests at Twyford Down, the A36/A350 Corridor Alliance comprises a number of local groups in South-West England historically concerned about the effects of proposed bypasses in their communities. The Alliance recognised that these would lead to a new superhighway along a corridor from Bristol to Southampton. Having succeeded in stopping most of the proposed road schemes, the Alliance continues to campaign against possible future plans for a strategic route from the M4 to the South Coast.